Pieces of Her

Her Life, Woven in Pieces of Love and Loss

Vishnu Priya.R

ISBN
Paperback 979-8-89724-056-2
Hardcase 979-8-89724-057-9

Contents

As I hold *Pieces of Her* in my hands, a journey that began deep within my soul, I am overwhelmed by the love and support that has carried me here. This book is not just a collection of words – it is a testament to the unwavering strength and inspiration that I have drawn from the most important people in my life. To each of you, my heart overflows with gratitude.

To my **Appa**, my guiding light in the darkest of times. When the world cloaked me in shadows, you saw the spark within me and nurtured it with your boundless love and sacrifices. Even when life tested you, you gave me everything I needed to shine. Your belief in me has been my greatest strength, and I owe so much of who I am to you. Thank you for being my hero, my anchor, and my endless source of hope.

To my **Amma**, my source of unconditional love and inspiration. You celebrate every small accomplishment of mine, no matter what the world says. Your pride in me, your unwavering support, and the love you shower upon me have been the wind beneath my wings. You teach me every day that love and kindness are the greatest gifts we can give. Thank you for always being proud of me, for standing by me, and for teaching me what it means to truly care.

To my sweet little sister, **Ammu**, my backbone and my safe haven. You know me inside and out, never judging, always understanding. At times, I wonder if you are my elder sister, with your wisdom, maturity, and clarity. You sit with me in my darkest hours, sharing my burdens and making my life infinitely brighter and easier. Thank you for being my confidante, my cheerleader, and my partner in everything. You are my pillar of strength, and I love you endlessly.

To my lovely **Latha Athai**, my sweet and caring aunt, who has always been proud of me and taught me the true meaning of unconditional love. Your warmth and faith in me have been a constant reminder of the beauty of familial bonds. Thank you for standing by me and being my haven of love and comfort.

And to **Allu**, who brought light to my journey in a different way. You inspired me to channel my traumas and joys into art, transforming pain into beauty and struggles into growth. You taught me the profound realities of life and the courage it takes to walk this path alone. Your presence in my life has been a source of inspiration and energy, and I am deeply grateful for the lessons and love you've shared.

To all of you, my four pillars and beyond – my lifeline, my everything. I don't often show it, but I wouldn't be who I am without you. You make my life better each day with your presence. Thank you for believing in me, for loving me, and for being there even when the world felt like it was crumbling. I love you all more than words can ever express.

This book is as much yours as it is mine. It is a reflection of the love, strength, and inspiration you have given me. Thank you for being the light in my life.

My Favourite Poem

Like gentle rain kissing,
the earth's face
I'll write all about you,
with endless grace
In each verse,
and every line
You're my cherished muse,
And I'll write for you endlessly
You are my favourite poem

My Choice

Among all the chaos,

The one thing I am dead certain about is 'YOU".

I am not sure what you did to make me fall in love with you!

I never thought I would choose you among all these perplexities

It's funny how deeply I feel for you without even knowing the reason.

Did you propose to me? NO

Did you promise me you'd stay with me forever? NO

Did you commit anything towards me? NO

Then why is my heart beating sooo fast when I think of you?

Among all the chaos, I am never exhausted to think about you

I don't expect you to commit to me or love me as I do

I just love you deeply for who you are

Even If we move apart permanently,

Even if I couldn't see you ever again,

Even if you love somebody else,

I will love you forever

Among all the uncertainties,

The one thing I am certain of is **YOU**.

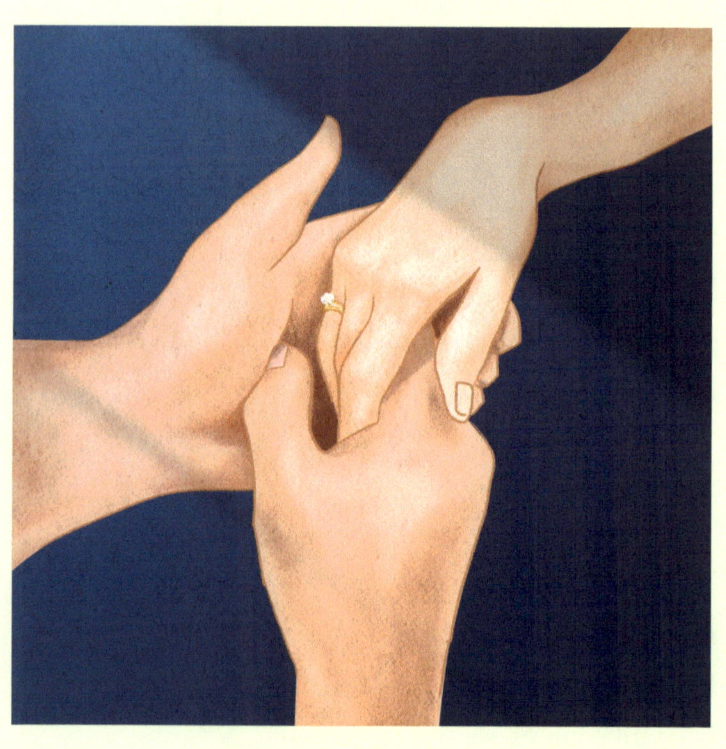

Temporary

I know you are afraid to get hurt all over again

You fear pain!!!

You fear the perplexed complexity of the situation

that might arise if we unite.

And you think I fell for you deeply because,

I haven't felt this much for anybody else?

Is that so?

Your exaggerated explanation about why we shouldn't unite,

makes me realise how much pain you must have experienced

before all this and how much you loved her

This is not your first time, and you have felt all these ecstatic feelings before

But this is my first time,

All the ecstatic flourishing feeling made me fall for you deep, real deep

and I am not afraid to feel hell for you, but again,

You remind me again and again that this is **TEMPORARY.**

Butterflies

I certainly do not feel the same excitement and butterflies,

When I am meeting other people

The amount of effort and love that I would pour out for you

cannot be attained by any people;

The thought of you Ignite fluttering butterflies in me

The love I feel for you cannot be bartered with any treasure in this world

You sprinkle little joys and lighten me in darkness

I would write a book about you, screaming the love I have for you

That's how I know I love you

That's how much I love you

The Imprints

Day by day,

My heart imprints the level of love I have for you

Even if I claim to be OK if you're gone,

I know I will miss you terribly!!!

Your unconditional love and trust towards me is,

Making me fall deeper in love with you

It might not be the same with you,

You might have prepared yourselves to leave me one day

But I am not prepared yet!!!

You are turning into this life source required for me,

To stay alive, to survive

But your physical presence is not my demand,

Your love, which is expressed in the most unconditional way,

Even when you're very far away, is enough for me

That's all I need

I Know

I know that I am neither your past nor your future

I know that I am so temporary as the seasons keep changing

I know I am just a passing cloud in your life

I know that I am not a non-negotiable priority in your life

I know that my efforts, time and love will evaporate like a dew drop in the sun

I know that my childish nature and attachment scare you

I know that all our most beautiful and magical moments are gonna be,

Just memories to you

I know that I'll be tagged as one of your lovers whom you fell in love with

accidentally and couldn't stay together due to so-called "SITUATIONS"

I know I will stay in the little corner of your mind forever

I know that somebody is gonna replace me and give you all the love

you'll ever need;

I know that you're gonna love somebody a little bit more than me,

I know that "OUR STORY" is gonna be just a love story to you in the end.

I am Scared

I am scared, yes! I am scared of losing all of you one day;

Even though I am aware that this is what's supposed to happen,

I am scared!!!

Your daily reminder of us not being in a "SERIOUS RELATIONSHIP",

makes me terrified!!!

I am scared that you're gonna leave me all alone,

I am scared that you're gonna move on from me like all your other relationships

I am scared that I am just your "ex" or not even qualified to be your "ex",

I am scared that I am gonna be completely ghosted and left out of your life!

I am scared that you're gonna love someone more than me

I am scared that one day we'll be completely nullified from each other's life matters

and be complete strangers

I am scared that you'll just forget me and erase me from your life

I am scared that I am gonna hold you so tight and never leave you,

Because I love you, and I don't wanna lose you!!!

I am scared that you'll be terrified of my attachment and love and

Drag me out of your life and close all the doors that I ever could get in

I am scared that you'll just be my beautiful dream

· · ·

Blindfold

You know!

You know that it hurts me

You know that you hurt me

And I am still hurting

Yet you choose to wear the blindfold :)

Now that I woke up from the delusion of your so-called "love",

Here you are demanding me to say "I love you", which I cannot!

The one thing I am gonna keep is my self-respect,

And I deny obeying your demands

Not anymore.

Expression

Do you know why I expect you to express,

Your love towards me constantly???

You might consider me as a needy, insecure, irritating

or maybe even a toxic person

But you need to understand this!

I need you to express your love or appreciation constantly

Because "that love you express" is like the food we eat,
the air we breathe to live.

We don't stop eating just because we ate yesterday, right?

We need food on a daily basis for energy and to live

and we don't stop breathing because we take in enough
oxygen;

We need air each and every second for survival

Likewise, your expression of love and your appreciation
is what

builds the relationship; it's like water to the plants

We need it, it's mandatory! Without it, we can die!!!

Even though I'm aware of your love towards me,

Expressing it is mandatory. Life is all about it!!!

It's small but certain happiness.

Just Another Girl

I may have acted up in a way you never expected me to

I may have crushed your belief that you could be,

horrifically open to me about anything!!!

I may have seemed like a toxic person to you

I may have acted so vulnerable in front of you, forgetting my limits

I may have thought you would understand

what's going on with me and persuade me!

I may have thought I was a very special person in your life,

with no room for secrecy

I may have thought I was your partner in crime

I may have thought you'd not be considering me, just like,

All the other girls you liked!!!

I may have thought you loved me unconditionally, vigorously!!!

Irrespective of all the promises and secrets you had in your life.

But again, you woke me up out of my trance and helped me realise that

I am just another girl.

Puzzling Mind

The human mind is funny and mysterious

At times, we misjudge the beautiful gift we have,

And underestimate their power and fall for,

the most manipulating, multifaceted illusionary gift

We are most likely to be heartbroken if we choose the second one,

And yet this funny, mysterious thing somehow;

tricks us and eats us inside and out

Finally, all that's gonna remain is the unmendable broken heart,

losing all the trust it ever had in love and the truth

Yes, I Would!

Yes! I am hopelessly madly in love with you

Yes! I fill my mind with all of you all the time

Yes! I smile like an idiot thinking about you

Yes! My pupil dilates, and my heart pounds

vigorously when I see you;

Yes! I imagine silly, dramatic and romantic

conversations with you in my head

Yes! I would get mad when any girl tries to,

Possess you or even think about it!

Yes! I would want to share each and every single,

Silly things about my day

Yes! I would want you to listen and understand;

My ranting about anything and everything

Yes! I would want to find new gazillion ways to love you and

keep our relationship exciting and mysterious

Yes! I would fight you and try to push you away at times;

So that you could persuade me;

Yes! I would dream about my sweet youth and peaceful

old age with you

Because no matter what you say,

I can't accept the fact that you'll leave me one day!

Wishful Love

I never intended to hide you from anyone,

In fact, I am eager to introduce you and express how,

extremely important and immensely special you are to me

I never wanted this to be just a story which fades away without,

being admired or inspired

I wanted our love to be stupendously phenomenal, magical and open;

So that the world is drawn and motivated to love like us

I want the world to look up to us!!!

I don't want the world to describe our love as "beautiful but unfinished love".

I wanted our story to be beautiful, irreplaceable and everlasting.

Attachment

The most terrifying thing that happened

I thought I was in control, but

it seems like I am not;

I am slowly drowning in my terror

This was not supposed to happen

I knew that I was in love, but

I didn't realise that I was deeply madly attached to you

Love can be blind and deep, but this

"attachment thing" is worse; it can kill me!

I am trying my best to distance myself from you, but it seems like,

I am gonna be killed; it's just a matter of time.

The Artist

I can't help but wonder

how much you have added to my life

It's normal to change in any way with new people in our lives;

But this, you have added so many colours to my life, which

I never thought existed in the first place.

Who are you?

How did you do this to me?

You have unlocked a new person inside of me

It's not that you have given me everything sunny and cosy,

But, you gave me storm and muddy pathways to walk through

Which made my comfort zone perish, and I flourished into,

The person who I am today

You unlocked the artist in me!!!

You will always be a part of me no matter where

and who you are with

This artist is gonna make you proud one day

Little Things

The little gifts we share,

The random pics we click

The unexpected sweet letters

The sweet flowers you give,

The sudden, surprising visits,

The daily mandatory little talks,

The mandatory good mornings and nights

The special trip on our birthdays,

Our own secret spots,

The untold understanding of feelings

The cute little DIY gifts we share

The effort made to see each other,

no matter how short of time we are!!!

The code language that we can only understand

The irritating topics that you bring up to make me possessive;

The urge to hug you tight,

for an adequate amount of time until you gasp for air

The hungry, craving eyes to meet you and fill all of you in me

The comfort my body and soul feel,

after wrapping myself in your clothes

is what makes us special!!!

All the little things are magic :)

You
can Do
Anything

Silly Me!

It might seem silly to you,

The gazillion pictures that I send you

The exact narration of the things that

happened in my day

The 100 calls I give you just to say, "I LOVE YOU."

The cute little poems I write for you,

The heartfelt letters I send you,

The mini music concert I perform for you.

The funny joker belly dance I learned for you

The morning prayers just for you,

Even though you don't believe in prayers

But it matters the most to me,

All these silly things are everything to me

You are everything to me

Compos Mentis

I can go on for days or even months without,

talking to you or meeting you

I can stop nagging you with all my silly little things

I can stop writing letters to you

I can be happy even if you avoid me,

as you are swamped in your work

I can be utterly contented with meeting you once in a while!

Do you know why?

That's because I'll whole-fully devote myself to you;

Doesn't matter if it's an hour or a minute

I will engulf all of you until I flow out

I'll celebrate each and every single second with you

I'll shower you with all the love I've got

I'll spoil you with all the good things I have for you,

That I can be contented for a lifetime

Each second with you will be spent like,

The last day of our lives

When your touch makes me feel like I am on fire,

I'll devour you like a lion devours its prey, but in a good way!

Thus, we live a lifetime in a very short time we meet.

Unchangeable

You left me,

And the silence screamed louder than words,

A void carved into my soul,

A wound no time can heal.

I trace your shadow in the cold,

In the hollow ache of empty rooms,

In the whispers of the wind,

That call your name as if to mock my grief.

I replay the moments,

The laughter like sunlit streams,

The touch that once anchored me,

Now, a ghost I cannot reach.

I begged the stars,

To rewrite the script of our story,

But they blinked indifferently,

Unmoved by my tears.

I screamed at the moon,

To turn back its tide,

But it only waned,

As if to echo my fading hope.

I tried to fix what broke,

To piece together shattered dreams,

But the cracks only deepened,

And your absence spoke louder than my efforts.

Now, I sit in the rubble of what we were,

Hands trembling, heart heavy,

Knowing there's nothing I can do,

To bring you back, to make you stay.

You are gone,

And I am left with the weight of forever,

Carrying a love that lingers,

Even as you fade into the distance.

• • •

The Weight of My Greed

I drank from the cup of your love,

Overflowing and pure,

But I never poured it back,

I let it drain, unmeasured, unsure.

Your hands built bridges to my heart,

While mine stayed idle, cold,

I basked in the warmth of your light,

Yet offered shadows to hold.

I took, and I took,

Every smile, every tender touch,

I swallowed your laughter like honey,

But I never gave as much.

You planted gardens in my barren soul,

Watered them with tears of devotion,

But I let weeds of neglect take root,

And drowned your love in my own ocean.

I was greedy, blind to the cost,

Your love was a treasure I thought I would never lose,

But treasures neglected turn to dust,

And now I'm left with only "was."

I saw you slip away,

A quiet storm, a gentle retreat,

And still, I clung to my selfish ways,

Until the silence was complete.

Now, I sit in the ruins,

Of a love I could not sustain,

The echoes of your whispered care,

A haunting, endless refrain.

I was rich, but I was foolish,

And now I understand too late,

Love demands to be cherished,

Or it succumbs to the weight.

The greed I carried has left me poor,

With nothing but regret's steady roar,

For I held the world in my careless hands,

And let it crumble like fragile sands.

The Light You Gave Me

I was a shadow, lost and cold,

A soul adrift, a story untold.

The night was my home, the silence my friend,

And I thought the darkness would never end.

But then you came, like a quiet flame,

Calling my name, easing my shame.

Your voice was a whisper, soft and kind,

A melody that woke my weary mind.

You reached for me with steady hands,

Pulled me from those desolate lands.

Your light broke through my shrouded skies,

A sunrise reflected in your gentle eyes.

I owe you more than words can say,

For chasing my shadows far away.

For teaching me how to feel the sun,

When I believed my battles couldn't be won.

You painted my world with bright colours,

Rekindled my hope, restored my sight.

You taught me to see the beauty I missed,

In every moment, in every twist.

I owe you my laughter, my every smile,

For walking with me that endless mile.

For showing me love, for showing me grace,

For being my anchor in life's vast space.

The darkness may call, but it holds no power,

For you've built me a home, a steadfast tower.

And forever in my heart, I'll keep,

The light you gave me, shining deep.

My Worth

It's true that I often forget your rule of not getting attached to each other

It's true that I am an amnesia patient when it comes to certain rules of yours

that are not to make you my first priority, which also means that I am not yours.

To not contact frequently so that I don't think you love me,

To not meet as often as possible to express our love, so that it doesn't make it feel official.

To not meet my simple needs, such as expressions of love, appreciation, or replies to my texts

which form the foundation of a relationship.

You don't introduce me to any of your special friends or family so that they don't mistake us for a couple.

You don't give me your emergency contact because you don't want me to be one.

You seem to love me and appreciate me in the dark with pride and contentment.

You are so proud of yourself for being 5000% brutally honest with me

Just because you are honest doesn't mean it's okay.

You fail to love me in the daylight as much as in the dark

But you never fail to mention the excruciating pain you have endured in your past,

which has consumed all your love for anything in the world.

You are frightened to get hurt & experience that excruciating pain from your past love

which makes me question my worth.

Yes! We know we can't be together forever

Yes, we can't officially marry.

But if you say you love me that much

Then why don't you give me the love that I deserve???

Am I not worth that excruciating pain?

All your rule books from your past

make me question my place in your life

What am I?

Am I just another girl you seemed to get attached to???

If yes, I am sorry! I am sorry to disappoint you.

I can't stay anymore.

I know the magic of my love,

I would want to give it to a soul who deserves it,

who understands it & loves it no matter what!!!

I Deserve More

I can swear that you are not just an infatuation or fling.

It's true that I did anything I could do to be with you,

to see you, to hear your voice, & to spend time with you.

Irrespective of how you claim you love me, that's not it.

You have never given me your love wholeheartedly.

I am not complaining, but if you are in love,

you surrender to that person, right?

To hell with your past stories and insecurities.

I deserve a person who can love me wholeheartedly as I do,

who can engulf me with love without losing the adventure & innocence.

Be My Sky

I want you to be like the sky.

It stays unapologetically itself,

Does it ever boast when there is a magnificent rainbow on it?

Like, "Hey, did you see my rainbow?"

Or does it apologise for dark, foggy, gloomy weather?

No, right???

Just like that, you don't have to be superior or feel inferior.

Just be "interior."

Be authentically yourself

and glow like you've swallowed the moon

The One

It might seem,

Like choices abound,

Yet it's a waste of time,

To chase 'the one,'

And spend a life

in endless rounds.

Ask yourself –

Why?

Do you truly seek

A relationship?

In your top 99?

Whether it's a mirage

Or something divine?

We humans, social beings,

Need company to survive,

Yes, we cherish solitude,

Yet crave warmth to thrive.

At the end of the day,

We lean on one another,

A pillar unyielding,

A soul to discover.

If only you'd see,

That "the one" you hold near,

Is all you need,

No need to steer

Into fleeting grass

Of greener hue,

For the lawn is lush

where love is true.

Humans are magic,

Made for connection.

Through love and care,

Through pure intention.

There's nothing as comforting

as living without the fear

that someone won't stay,

That love will disappear.

Through trials and death,

Through seasons and pain,

May you find "the one,"

And love's refrain.

One Day

One day, I asked him,
"How do you see me with someone else?"
He softly said,
"Seeing you with someone else is my helplessness,
But knowing that what was between us
Happens only once in a lifetime
Is my pride."
I know that you are happy with her,
But I believe we had our good share of happiness.
You were the one who used to say,
"It is better to be ignorant than to know the truth."
That's why I don't see you with anyone else.
When you are with me,
I consider you only mine,
Because I can't help it.
I have tried staying away from you,
I have also tried to be with someone else.
But this love is way beyond passion.
I have even tried hating you,
I have tried living without you,
I have tried seeing you with someone else.
But when I see you with someone else,
I see myself.

The Chase

I want him because he doesn't want me,
A twisted longing, yet it sets me free.
Place me in a room of love's warm embrace,
I'll seek the cold, the indifferent face.

Convincing the distant, proving my worth,
A cycle I've spun since my earliest birth.
Deep-rooted wounds, therapy's plea,
But I'll text him instead and wait helplessly.

It's not that I shun love's tender hue,
Believe me, I crave it through and through.
But childhood taught me a lesson: unkind,
That love is earned, not freely assigned.

The chase is addictive, a habit ingrained,
A pattern of longing that keeps me chained.
I want him because he doesn't want me,
And he knows it too – that's his guarantee.

One-Sided Love

I asked him one day, "Your love is one-sided,

Yet you hold on – why not be divided?"

He smiled and said, "Loving you this way,

Means loving all of you, come what may.

The part of you I cherish, the part that's free,

Even the part that cannot love me.

My one-sided love liberates my heart,

From the chains of expectations relationships impart.

For one-sided love knows no reason or aim,

No conditions, no purpose, no need to claim.

It's a war I fight, knowing I'll lose,

Yet I march on, for it's the path I choose."

Right Person, Wrong Time

One day, he asked me, with sorrowed eyes,
"Was it necessary to say goodbye?"
I replied, "I never wanted to leave this way,
Never wanted to face the world astray.

I dreamed of fighting over trivial things,
Of the lifelong bond such conflict brings.
But sometimes endings don't mean a break;
They're just the closure we're meant to take.

So this time, you have to let me go,
A lesson in love, a truth we both know.
Perhaps I'm the right person, wrong time,
The right collision, but the road's misaligned.

Our stories are perfect, yet something feels wrong,
Right chapters, but the characters don't belong."

A Love You'll Never Know

You'll never know that I love you so,

I hide it well; it will never show.

I'm a good liar, no one can tell,

This secret of mine, I guard it well.

It feels so safe, just in my head,

Where love is alive, yet words go unsaid.

I like the idea, this silent refrain,

Where love is pure, untouched by pain.

You won't break my heart, not this time,

If only I love you within my mind.

A quiet solace, no need to confess,

A love unspoken, yet no less.

The Strength in Sensitivity

You call me sensitive, weak, and frail,
Fragile and foolish when tears set sail.
But you don't see the strength it takes,
To bare my soul, though my heart aches.

To be sensitive is to feel it all,
The joy, the sorrow, each rise and fall.
It's loving fiercely, with all my might,
Embracing the dark and chasing the light.

My vulnerability, a gift to you,
A love so pure, raw, and true.
Breaking my walls is no easy feat,
Yet I do it for you, my love complete.

But if my sensitive walls rise tall,
And I stand fierce, unyielding to all,
That's when you'll know, with no more to prove,
We are done, and I've nothing to lose.

In A Hurry

I don't have time to fight or feud,

To envy, gossip, or misconstrue.

No space for hate, no need to compare,

No chase for perfection, no need to declare.

Life is fleeting, I've come to see,

There's no second chance for you or me.

Each second now holds the utmost worth,

A treasure trove while I walk this earth.

I choose to laugh, to cry, to share,

To love, be kind, and show I care.

To live with gratitude, to find my peace,

And cherish life's gift before it must cease.

Always With Me

The way my heart aches to share with you,

Every beautiful sight, every radiant hue.

It races fast as if I've flown,

Knowing these wonders would feel like home.

In journeys, I take, where you're not near,

I fill the silence with memories clear.

Collecting moments, like fragile art,

To carry you with me, etched in my heart.

So know this truth, though we're apart,

You're always with me, a constant spark.

In every breath, in all I see,

You're the beauty that lives within me.

Love from Afar

I will never call you a friend,
For in your eyes, those nights ascend.
My dreams once carved your face so true,
Now that face belongs to someone new.

This choice you've made, I can't pretend,
To love so close, to love as friends.
From far, I'll hold my heart's embrace,
Yet, I wonder: Will she see my trace?

Will you show her the mark that I knew?
The stories it held, the laughter too?
When you drink deep and gaze at the moon,
Won't echoes of us make your heart swoon?

If we meet by chance, will you stray?
Find reasons for closeness and words to convey.
Can friendship bloom, pure and bright,
When love still lingers, haunting the night?

A Question of Friendship?

The mark on your waist, will she ever see?

Will she know its tale or what it meant to me?

When your thoughts blur and shadows blend,

Will you remember how we'd never end?

When the moonlight spills, soft and wide,

Will you think of me by your side?

If paths should cross, will you stand still,

Or let your heart betray your will?

Can friendship live where love once burned,

Where every glance feels like a return?

This bond, you ask, I cannot mend,

For love can't shrink to fit as a "friend."

Unstoppable Together

New Year's night, a wish unspoken,
I thought our bond was long since broken.
But there you stood, to my surprise,
Bringing light back to my tear-filled skies.

A stranger, I thought, after our fight,
Yet you proved me wrong that magical night.
You embraced me whole, without a doubt,
And silenced the fears I carried about.

As the clock struck twelve, time stood still,
Two souls as one, bound by will.
You in me, and I in you,
A world so vast, yet just us two.

Unstoppable, together we soar,
A love so fierce, it shakes the core.
No force can break what we've become,
For in your arms, I've found my home.

#sutulu

Genuine Love

No one could love you as I do,
With a heart so steadfast, pure, and true.
Through every storm, I'd stand and stay,
A lighthouse guiding you on your way.

No fleeting spark, no shallow flame,
My love endures, it knows no shame.
In every glance, in every sigh,
A boundless depth you can't deny.

Others may come, others may go,
But none will feel the way I know.
For in my soul, your name is carved,
A timeless art, perfectly starved.

No one will hold your broken parts,
Or stitch the wounds within your heart,
Like me, who sees your every scar,
You're my universe, my guiding star.

So when the world feels cold and bare,

Remember the love that's always there.

No one could ever love you as I,

For you are my earth, my sea, my sky.

#luttuz

...

A Vow Renewed

I'll do it all: the dreams we drew,

The plans we made, just me and you.

Each promise whispered, I now embrace,

For I've learned the cost of love's misplaced grace.

Failed words once carved a chasm wide,

But now I kneel with truth as my guide.

I've felt the ache of love that's lost,

And won't pay that heavy cost again.

The risk of losing you once more

is a pain my heart cannot endure.

So here I stand, steadfast and true,

To honour the vows I made to you.

Every moment, each desire,

I'll light them all with love's pure fire.

For losing you would break my soul,

And with you, I am finally whole.

A Promise of Forever

I'll make your time on earth divine,

Each moment precious, wholly mine.

No shadow shall linger, no fear take hold,

For I'll guard your heart with love untold.

I'll walk beside you, come what may,

Through trials and dreams, night or day.

Your goals will bloom, your hopes will soar,

As I lift you higher, forevermore.

I'll weave your days with joy and light,

Turn every wrong into something right.

I'll stand as your shield, your fiercest defender,

A love so pure, steadfast and tender.

You'll never face the dark alone,

In my embrace, you've found your home.

Together, we'll craft a life well-spent,

Filled with purpose, peace, and content.

So trust in me, for I am here,

To make your path bright and clear.

Your journey on earth, I'll make sublime,

A masterpiece etched in the sands of time.

The Pieces of Me

The pieces of me, scattered and torn,
A mosaic of light and shadows worn.
I am everything, yet I am none,
A fleeting echo, a rising sun.

I've often wondered, in quiet despair,
Would I love myself if I weren't here?
Would I embrace the chaos I bring,
Or see only cracks in this fragile being?

But then there's you, so steady, so kind,
Seeing beauty in what I can't find.
Even when I change, from day to day,
You love me still in every way.

You know me deeper than I dare,
Unravelling truths, I'm too scared to bear.
And in your hands, so gentle, so wise,
You hold my dreams and help them rise.

For you've paved a path, soft and bright,
Guiding my heart through the darkest night.
With every step, I feel your grace,
Turning my doubts into a sacred space.

So here I stand, both broken and whole,
Grateful to you for mending my soul.
The pieces of me you've taught to sing,
A symphony now to everything.

Abandoned

You left me,
like a diseased stray,
as if my one mistake
had claws sharp enough
to tear through the bond
we once called unbreakable.
I begged,
Not with pride,
But with the rawness of a heart
crushed by its own folly.
I knelt at the altar of your ego,
Praying for absolution,
Only to find your back
turned in cold dismissal.
Was my love so fragile,
that it shattered with a single crack?
Was your anger so fierce,
it drowned the whispers
of every promise we made,
every sacred memory

we built together?
I am left burning,
consumed by the fire
you kindled with your indifference.
You gave up all we had,
The laughter, the tears,
The moments when the world
was nothing but us,
In honour of your pride,
Your vengeance.
What am I to you?
A fleeting distraction,
a reprieve from the shadows
of your own confused,
procrastinated existence?
Was I ever more than a crutch
for your lonely nights,
a balm for your restless soul?
Tell me,
how do I trust again?
When the hands
I once reached for in despair
became the ones
that let me fall.
In the ashes of this betrayal,

I search for an answer,

but all I find is silence.

A silence heavier

than any goodbye.

The Weight of One Mistake

You cast me away,

like a diseased, forsaken dog,

as if my plea for forgiveness

were knives against your skin.

I knelt before the altar of your pride,

hands trembling,

heart bleeding,

for one misstep, one crack in the glass,

while the shards of our promises

still gleamed with yesterday's light.

How do I trust

a love that turns its back,

like the closing of a heavy door,

like vengeance disguised as virtue?

You held the torch,

not to guide me,

but to set me aflame,

watching as I burned

with the weight of your anger.

Was I merely a distraction?

A fleeting shadow

in the chaos of your lonely,

hesitant, wandering life?

Did I hold no value

beyond the comfort of your need?

You honoured your ego,

your fury,

above the fragile temple we built.

Brick by brick, moment by moment,

all discarded,

for what?

I am no saint,

but neither am I ash.

Yet here I stand,

haunted,

asking the hollow echoes:

What am I to you?

A memory,

or just the mistake

you could never forgive?

• • •

Numb

I sit here,

your presence a shadow

that once felt like home.

Now, it suffocates,

a weight pressing on my chest,

leaving me numb.

You abandoned me,

Not just in action,

But in soul,

Like a discarded page

of a story unfinished,

a mistake too heavy

for your pride to bear.

You made me beg,

made me cry,

made me unravel

into something unrecognisable.

I played the fool,

kneeling at the altar of your ego,

offering my tears

as if they could cleanse

the stain of my imperfection.
And when you finally spoke
words of forgiveness
dripping with false grace,
Did you feel mighty?
Did your pride swell
As I bowed,
broken and small,
beneath the weight of your gaze?
But here's the truth:
I regret it.
I pity myself
for pleading,
for believing
that what we had
was worth the humiliation.
I see it now,
The moment you left me
to burn in my own despair,
Our precious "us"
was reduced to ashes.
We act normal,
like nothing has changed.
But I'm not the same,
you're not the same,

we are not the same.
This is a ghost,
a facade we wear
to hide the hollow truth:
we died that day.
You never loved me,
Not the way I thought.
It wasn't love,
but fleeting attraction,
a fire that burned bright
until my flaw snuffed it out.
And now, here we are,
pretending,
because it's easier
than facing the emptiness
you left behind.
But I am relieved,
relieved to know the truth:
you were never mine,
and I was never yours.
This, whatever it is,
is not alive.
It's just echoes,
lingering in a place
we should have left behind.

Illusion

I've fallen,
not into the arms of love,
but into the abyss
of what I thought it was.
A coma of your so-called affection,
a dream so vivid
I mistook it for truth.
You warned me.
You said,
"I can't love you

The Coma

I am lost in the coma
of what I called love,
a dream spun from your warnings
and my stubborn heart.
You told me:
You can't love me the way I need.
But I didn't listen.
I painted over your words
with colors of hope,
crafting a masterpiece of lies
I called "us."
I built a world in your shadow,
a fragile illusion
where every glance you gave
was devotion,
every fleeting touch
a promise.
Reality whispered its truth,
but I buried it
beneath the weight

of my longing.
You stood firm,
unwavering,
your honesty as clear
as the sky before a storm.
And yet I chose blindness,
sinking deeper into the pit
of my own creation.
I loved the idea of you,
the reflection of who I thought
you could be.
But now the dream is broken,
and I am left
with the jagged shards
of what never was.
Your love was a warning,
not a gift,
and I was a fool
to make it more.
I see it now:
The emptiness in your touch,
The truth in your silence.
You were honest
and I was blind.
Now, I sit in the ruins

of a love that never lived,

Finally awake,

But still aching

for the dream.

The End of Us

It's over now,

The threadbare illusion of hope

I wove for you

has unravelled.

The tapestry of unconditional love

I bled to create

lies in tatters,

and all I see

is a desert,

parched and lifeless,

where only the cactus survives,

its spines sharp

with the bitterness you left me.

You made me this.

This barren heart,

this hardened soul.

What shall I do?

You held me like a plaything,

a cute distraction,

A puppy to amuse you,

But never the lifeline

you'd fight to hold.
You gave up on me.
You handed me over
to the rules you worship,
to the family you idolize,
to the society
that drains you dry.
As if their approval
could ever nourish you,
as if their hollow praise
could ever fill
the void of losing me.
You lost me, dear.
You'll understand it someday.
When the weight of their rules
feels like chains
around your soul,
when the echoes of my love
haunt the empty spaces
you can no longer fill,
you'll see.
It's just a matter of time.
I will make you see,
Not through vengeance,
But through absence.

Through the silence

of what could have been,

through the ache

of knowing you let go

of something real.

And I will walk away,

scarred but stronger,

leaving you

to the desert you chose,

while I find my way

to greener shores.